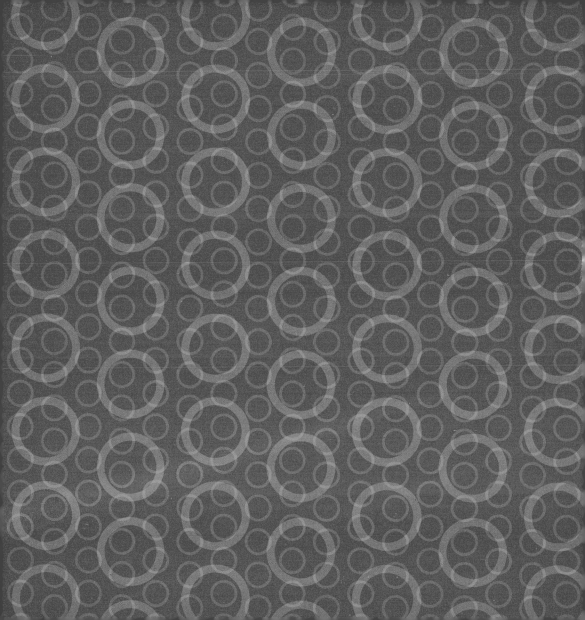

212°

SERVICE

THE 10 RULES FOR CREATING A SERVICE CULTURE

BY MAC ANDERSON

212° **SERVICE**—The 10 Rules for Creating a Service Culture

Table of Contents

INTRODUCTION

There's a law of science that could change the way you think about service:

At 211 degrees, water is hot.
At 212 degrees, it boils.
With boiling water, comes steam.
And steam can power a locomotive.

AND...IT'S THAT
ONE EXTRA DEGREE

that makes all the difference!

That's what this little book is all about...how that one extra degree of service can take your organization's culture from good to great!

Someone once said, "Life is like a game of tennis. The player who serves well seldom loses." The same can be said for any business on the planet.

However, in business, when we talk about creating a service culture, most people will focus on "customer service." But 212° service defines a service culture a little differently. In addition to serving the customers, it is also about serving each other. In fact, you'll learn it's impossible to have one without the other.

From day one, my goal at Simple Truths has been to create a service culture, and I'm proud to say…I think we have. Each new employee will hear the same speech when I say, "**You must always remember you're not here to serve me…I'm here to serve you. I'm here to give you the tools, the resources and the products to convert our customers into 'raving fans.'** In addition, my job is to create an atmosphere where we'll want to serve each other with a smile in our hearts, because, that's the only way this will be a great place to work!"

There are many books written about service; many good ones, in fact. However, my goal in this one is to keep it simple…to present ten rules which I consider the most important on your road to success. Rules presented in a simple, but engaging way that you and your team can read in less than 30 minutes. And when you're finished, say…**"Wow, we can do this!"**

However, I would never suggest that creating a service culture is easy. It's not. Anything worthwhile never is. But my challenge to you is to put these ten rules to the test, and if you do, you'll discover a workplace filled with passion, respect, kindness and fun.

Here's to your quest for 212° service.

Mac Anderson
Founder, Simple Truths

RULE #

It Starts at the Top

Rule #1 for creating a service culture or any culture for that matter is this: It starts at the top. It starts in the head and the heart of the leader and is passed on from one team member to the next. There is no other way it can happen.

"You can't teach culture. You have to live it. You have to experience it. You have to share it. You have to show it." These are words from Brent Harris, a top executive for Nordstrom, the retail chain known for legendary service.

To change any culture, in any company, the people at the top have to live it! Because words without deeds mean nothing!

When Dave Neeleman started the airline JetBlue, he knew the importance of leading from the front and letting his actions speak louder than words. His mission was to create a customer service culture, and he knew all eyes would be watching.

A few years ago, I read a great story in *INC. Magazine* written by Norm Brodsky. In it, Brodsky wrote about being on a JetBlue flight when Neeleman was on board. *As we were buckling up to take off, Neeleman stood up and introduced himself,* "Hi, I'm Dave Neeleman, the CEO of JetBlue. I'm here to serve you today and I'm looking forward to meeting every one of you before we land."

As he was handing out snack

"GOOD LEADERS MUST FIRST BECOME GOOD SERVANTS."
— ROBERT K. GREENLEAF

14

212 SERVICE STRATEGY

TO CHANGE A
CULTURE
THE PEOPLE AT THE
TOP HAVE TO LIVE IT.

baskets he would stop to chat with everyone. When he came to me, I told him I thought it was a great idea to service his customers first-hand, and asked him how often he did it. Expecting him to say once or twice a year, he said, "Not often enough…I get to do it about once a month."

Out of curiosity, I watched him interact with other passengers. In several instances, I saw him taking notes and listening intently to what passengers were saying. In a few instances when he couldn't answer the question, I watched him take a business card and say, "Someone will be in touch with you in the next 24 hours." Even at the end of the flight, there was Neeleman, in his blue apron, leading the charge collecting the trash from the seat pockets.

Now, here's a question for you…**Is there any doubt that JetBlue employees knew that their leader was willing to walk the talk when it came to serving the customers? And is there any doubt that the front line knew he was on their team?**

When asked if he thought leading by example was the most important quality of leadership, the great humanitarian, Albert Schweitzer thought for a second, and then replied,

"NO, IT'S NOT THE MOST IMPORTANT ONE.
IT'S THE ONLY ONE."

So, what about you? Are you a servant leader?

Are you committed to serving both your customers and your employees—to creating an atmosphere where employees WANT to do their best for customers?

 A few years ago, I was invited to spend some time with Ken Blanchard at his lake home in upstate New York. Over the last 20 years, Ken has probably sold more books than any other business author. His classic, *The One Minute Manager*, has sold more than 10 million copies. He has also built a large training company with the focus on servant leadership and customer service.

I've had the good fortune to meet many successful business people, authors and speakers during my career, but I've never met

"HAPPINESS...
CONSISTS IN GIVING,
AND IN
SERVING
OTHERS."

— HENRY DRUMMOND

anyone who "walked the talk" more than Ken. He gets it. The first night of my visit to Ken's lake home, we were sitting on the deck with Humberto, his son-in-law, talking about some ways we could work together. It was about 10 p.m., when all of a sudden Ken jumped up and asked to be excused. He returned about 10:20 and Humberto asked, "What happened?"

Ken said, "I can't believe it; I forgot to call Dorothy on her birthday."

Later that night, after Ken had gone to bed, Humberto told me that Dorothy is an 85-year-old, part-time employee for the company. It then dawned on me that at 10 p.m., Ken left to spend almost 20 minutes talking to Dorothy and inquiring about how she had spent her special day. However, after spending more time with Ken over the next year, I came to realize that this was no fluke. This is who he is.

The last time while visiting him at his San Diego office, I learned that one of his employees who worked in the warehouse had recently passed away. Ken had invited the employee's wife to come to his office.

212° SERVICE STRATEGY

LOOK ACTIVELY FOR
OPPORTUNITIES
TO THANK AND
REWARD YOUR PEOPLE

BECOME A SERVANT LEADER, LEAD FROM YOUR HEART.

212° SERVICE

When she arrived, he spent an hour walking around with her carrying a tape recorder to record all of the wonderful memories that other employees had of her husband. When the wife left, she said it was a day she'd never forget.

> You see, what many leaders would have considered a waste of time, Ken saw as an opportunity to serve and to thank his people. He doesn't do it because it's expected of him, he does it because he truly cares. It comes from the heart, and his people love him for being the servant leader that he is.

This is an old Chinese poem that offers wonderful advice for any leader:

GO to the people
LIVE among the people
LEARN from them
LOVE them.
START with what they know,
BUILD on what they have.
But of the **BEST** leaders,
When their **TASK** is accomplished,
Their **WORK** is done,
The **PEOPLE** will remark,

"WE HAVE DONE IT OURSELVES."

RULE #

YOUR CUSTOMERS MUST COME SECOND

Your Customers Must Come Second

It's like the chicken or the egg question… Who comes first if you want to achieve business success—your customers or your employees? Herb Kelleher, one of the founders and former CEO of Southwest Airlines—an industry leader in customer service, sheds some light on the answer:

"I always felt that our people came first. Some of the business schools regarded that as a conundrum. **They would say: Which comes first, your people, your customers, or your shareholders?** And I would say, it's not a conundrum. Your people come first, and if you treat them right, they'll treat the customers right, and the customers will come back, and that'll make the shareholders happy."

So what's the first step?

HIRE THE BEST PEOPLE...AND TREAT THEM RIGHT!

Howard Schultz, Starbucks' founder, understood that the key to the success of his then fledgling coffee business was to recruit well-educated people who were eager to communicate their passion for coffee. This, he felt, would be his competitive advantage in an industry where turnover was 300 percent a year. To hire the best people, he also knew he must be willing to pay them more than the going wage and offer health

benefits that weren't available elsewhere. He saw that part-time people made up two-thirds of his employee base, and no one in the restaurant industry offered benefits to part-timers. Schultz went to work in an effort to sell his board of directors on increasing expenses while most restaurant executives in the 1980s were looking for ways to cut costs. Initially Starbucks was still losing money. But Schultz was persistent. He was looking long term and was committed to growing the business with passionate people. He won, and he said many times afterwards that this decision was one of the most important decisions, if not the most important, that he had made at Starbucks. His employee retention rate was about five times the industry average, but more importantly, he could attract people with great attitudes who made their customers feel welcome and at home.

When hiring someone, start with the premise that attitudes are contagious. Then ask yourself one question...Is theirs worth catching?

I've been in business for over 30 years and I've come to realize the difference in success and failure is not how you look, not how you dress, not how much you're educated, but

HOW YOU THINK!

In my business life, I've watched many very intelligent people fail miserably because they have a negative attitude, and I've also observed just as many people with average intelligence soar to success because of positive attitudes.

Southwest Airlines' VP of People is often asked the question, How do you get your people to be so nice? Her answer is always the same…

"WE HIRE NICE PEOPLE."

It sounds almost too simple to be important, but "hiring nice people" has been the cornerstone of their amazing success in a highly competitive industry. They understand their competitors may be able to match their price and copy their business model; however, they feel that the spirit and the attitude of their employees will be extremely difficult to replicate.

"YOUR
ATTITUDE
WILL DETERMINE

YOUR
ALTITUDE."

— ZIG ZIGLAR

RULE #

Engage the Hearts and Minds of Your Employees

RULE # 3

"When something captures your heart, you are driven to succeed. Heartpower is the very core of any successful enterprise. Capture the heart, and you have captured the employee. For without a vibrant, beating heart, any enterprise is sure to die."

— **Jim Harris**

Engage both the minds…and the hearts of your employees…and watch your company soar. It all starts with creating a compelling vision…one that focuses on your mission to serve.

Here's how Jim Harris, author of *Getting Employees to Fall in Love with Your Company*, explains it:

"To capture the hearts of our employees, it is essential that we tell them what we stand for and where we are going. Our vision must be compelling, understandable, and focused.

"As Bill Wiggenhorn, president of Motorola University, reminds us (and this may come as a shock to many financial managers), the so-called

212 SERVICE STRATEGY

A VISION MUST BE COMPELLING, UNDERSTANDABLE AND FOCUSED

vision of 'Shareholder Equity, Rah! Rah! Rah! doesn't get people out of bed each day.' When Dr. Martin Luther King, Jr., spoke to 500,000 civil rights marchers in front of the Lincoln Memorial, he did not exclaim, 'I have a strategic plan today.' Dr. King, understanding the power of a compelling vision, enthusiastically proclaimed, 'I have

"YOU GET THE **BEST EFFORTS** FROM OTHERS NOT BY LIGHTING A FIRE BENEATH THEM, BUT BY **BUILDING A FIRE WITHIN."**

— Bob Nelson

a dream today,' which became the focus of the entire civil rights movement."

Capturing your vision in a way that's easily understood is a powerful call to action. It's the foundation of your company—a way to share your mission to serve.

We can all take a lesson about creating an easy-to-understand vision from United Supermarkets. This award-winning, service-oriented grocery chain based in Texas, summarized its mission in just six words:

It's simple, easy to remember and an invitation to the pursuit of excellence. Your company's mission is a statement about what you stand for and where you are going—it is your ship's rudder.

But, however you define your mission, it's not just about the words you choose. Too often company mission statements are agonized over and then forgotten in a binder somewhere.

To make your values come alive, you have to live them…and give your employees the tools to make them a reality.

United Supermarkets' CEO Dan Sanders explains it this way:

"This vision, this purpose, these values, become impregnated into the very soul of the community, of the entire culture. Everyone feels accountable to them and accountable to each other… Everyone possesses this value system and common belief about working toward a shared vision and mission to serve.

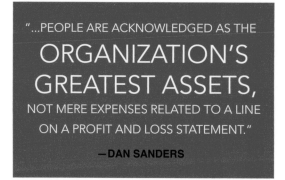

"…PEOPLE ARE ACKNOWLEDGED AS THE **ORGANIZATION'S GREATEST ASSETS,** NOT MERE EXPENSES RELATED TO A LINE ON A PROFIT AND LOSS STATEMENT."

—DAN SANDERS

"A sustainable culture is built from the inside out. It starts with leadership that places the highest level of importance on human beings and a corresponding premium on recruiting, hiring, and training—both academic and experiential training—to equip and empower them. People are acknowledged as the organization's greatest assets, not mere expenses related to a line on a profit and loss statement."

Creating a people-centered culture engages your staff and captures their hearts. Think about integrating the following into the fabric of your company:

| CREATING OPEN, TWO-WAY COMMUNICATION | LETTING PEOPLE MAKE DECISIONS | SHARING ECONOMIC RESULTS THROUGH PROFIT SHARING OR GAINS SHARING | INVESTING IN TRAINING AND DEVELOPMENT |

Whatever fits within your company's budget and culture, the bottom line is this:

MAKE YOUR WORKPLACE FEEL LIKE A FAMILY.

Remembering the Golden Rule at work will go a long way toward making employees feel valued for the unique contributions they make every day.

RULE #

MAKE YOUR
CULTURE
YOUR BRAND

Make Your Culture Your Brand

RULE #

You can't argue with success.

And there haven't been too many companies that have experienced such a meteoric rise as the online retailer, Zappos.com. The company grew to $1 billion in gross revenue in ten years and was the highest-ranking newcomer in *Fortune* magazine's annual "Best Companies to Work For" list in 2009.

In his book, *Delivering Happiness…A Path to Profits, Passion, and Purpose*, Zappos CEO Tony Hsieh outlines the importance of making your culture your brand…and its impact on customer service.

"At Zappos.com, we decided a long time ago that we didn't want our brand to be just about shoes, or clothing, or even online retailing. We decided that we wanted to build our brand to be about the very best customer service and the very best customer experience. We believe that customer service shouldn't be just a department, it should be the entire company.

"What's the best way to build a brand for the long term? In a word:

"At Zappos, our belief is that if you get the culture right, most of the other stuff—like great customer service, or building a great long-term brand, or passionate employees and customers—will happen naturally on its own.

"We believe that your company's culture and your company's brand are really just two sides of the same coin. The brand may lag the culture at first, but eventually it will catch up.

"YOUR CULTURE IS YOUR BRAND."

At Zappos, every employee, regardless of title or department, attends a four-week training program that covers the company's history, the importance of customer service, the long-term vision of the company, and the philosophy of company culture. Then it's off to take phone calls from customers for two weeks.

In fact, for an online company, Zappos is focused on creating an unparalleled customer experience, not over the Internet...but on the phone. Rather than being measured by the number of calls they take in a day, or being forced to up-sell, Zappos call center representatives focus on developing a personal emotional connection and building a lifelong relationship with each customer, one phone call at a time.

Companies like Zappos, and others with histories of legendary service, focus on maximizing the customer experience.

In another example, Nordstrom, despite their success, continues to project an image of small town modesty and humility. They say

"EVERYONE CAN BE GREAT...
BECAUSE
EVERYONE CAN
SERVE."

— MARTIN LUTHER KING, JR.

42

there is nothing magical about what they do and that their system is embarrassingly simple. "We outservice, not outsmart" is a typical Nordstromism. They rarely talk about themselves. **"We can't afford to boast. If we did, we might start to believe**

NORDSTROM MANTRA

WE OUTSERVICE, NOT OUTSMART

our own stories and quit trying to get better." In fact, when Bruce Nordstrom was selected as "Man of the Year" by *Footwear News*, he politely declined to be interviewed.

> **"It's not about us," said Bruce's son, Blake, who described the role of his family members as "stewards of the business culture."**

Nordstrom gives its employees the latitude they need to do what's right for the customer. Therefore, it should be no surprise that Nordstrom has always been known for their exceptional customer service.

The Nordstrom employee handbook reflects the culture they have created. Here's what it says (a total of 75 words):

Welcome to Nordstrom

*We're glad to have you with our Company. Our number one goal is to provide **outstanding customer service**. Set both your personal and professional goals high. We have great confidence in your ability to achieve them.*

Our employee handbook is very simple. We have only one rule...

Use good judgment in all situations.

Please feel free to ask your Department Manager, Store Manager or Human Resource office any question at any time.

What can I say except...

LESS IS ALMOST ALWAYS MORE.

RULE #

UNDERSTAND THE
"HOW OF
WOW"

RULE # **5**

Forget about just satisfying

your customers; you need Raving Fans! According to Ken Blanchard and Sheldon Bowles, who wrote *Raving Fans*, the difference is that raving fans, unlike satisfied customers, become part of your sales force. They tell friends, family and co-workers about your service and your products. And, of course, good things happen.

With the immediacy and viral capability of social media such as Facebook, Twitter, or Yelp, falling short of an opportunity to create "Raving Fans" can easily backfire—starting a negative tidal wave of publicity.

So, tell everyone in your organization to go beyond just satisfying customers…they need to create RAVING FANS! It may seem like a little thing, but this new mindset will make a big difference in building a service culture that can separate you from your competition.

THE HOW OF WOW — ONE SIMPLE RULE: ## CONSISTENCY COUNTS

In his book, *Hug Your Customers*, Jack Mitchell, CEO of a Connecticut-based clothing retailer, shares the importance of consistency in "Wowing your Customers:"

"Winning teams perform at their best day in and day out. They're consistent. It means delivering exceptional customer service the first time you encounter a customer, then doing it again the second time and the third time and the fortieth time.

"ALWAYS GIVE THE CUSTOMER MORE THAN THEY EXPECT."

— NELSON BOSWELL

"Consistency is very important in any business. It's why McDonald's is so fussy that its french fries are made identically at every franchise, every day. And if you deliver the same high level of service on your busiest days as you do on your quietest days, it really impresses customers. That has to be your goal."

Now, we all know that since businesses are staffed by human beings, mistakes will happen. **But mistakes are really opportunities to learn something new and to make adjustments to your service.**

212 SERVICE STRATEGY

PEOPLE DON'T CARE ABOUT HOW MUCH YOU KNOW UNTIL THEY KNOW HOW MUCH YOU CARE.

These 10 phrases from my friends at Walk the Talk are an illuminating reminder of how uncomplicated it is to give customers more than they expect. People don't care how much you know, (or what you sell, or what type of service you provide) until they know how much you care!

10 SERVICE PHRASES YOU SHOULD KNOW

10 *The* TEN *most important words:*

"I APOLOGIZE FOR OUR MISTAKE. LET ME MAKE IT RIGHT."
When something goes wrong, most people just want to be heard and acknowledged. So listen, apologize, then ask what you can do to make it right.

9 *The* NINE *most important words:*

"THANK YOU FOR YOUR BUSINESS. PLEASE COME BACK AGAIN."
Repeat customers cost less than new customers and are often more loyal.

8 *The EIGHT most important words:*

"I'M NOT SURE, BUT I WILL FIND OUT."
It's ok if you don't know the answer; it's not ok to make the customer keep searching for it. That's your job.

7 ***The SEVEN most important words:***

"WHAT ELSE CAN I DO FOR YOU?"
Be prepared to go the extra mile;
there is less competition there.

6 ***The SIX most important words:***

"WHAT IS MOST CONVENIENT FOR YOU?"
Your customers will be pleasantly surprised when you ask
what's convenient for them.

5 ***The FIVE most important words:***

"HOW MAY I SERVE YOU?"
This question reinforces your role in the relationship.
Play that role the best you can.

4 ***The FOUR most important words:***

"HOW DID WE DO?"
Feedback is critical! Your customers have a unique
perspective and they appreciate being asked.

3 **The THREE most important words:**

"GLAD YOU'RE HERE!"
Customers who feel welcome spend more time, more money and are more likely to return.

2 **The TWO most important words:**

"THANK YOU."
Basic manners...but how often do you get thanked when you're the customer?

1 **The MOST important word:**

"YES."
Become a yes person.

"A Crash Course on Customer Service" is from *180 Ways to Walk the Customer Service Talk* by Eric Harvey.

Here are some other examples that will get you thinking about the "How of Wow:"

In *Positively Outrageous Service,* T. Scott Gross tells us how easy it can be to add something to your service equation—something small that creates a lasting impression, loyal customers, and terrific word-of-mouth, while costing your company next to nothing:

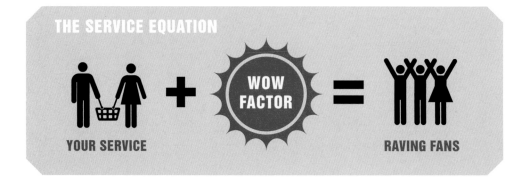

First-time visitors to a restaurant famed for its desserts are amazed to find a generous and totally unexpected slab of delicious cake tucked in with their take-home leftovers. As a result, many have become regular customers and have brought in dozens of friends over the years.

How about these from Jim Williamson in his book, *Service: Lessons Learned?*

 A Kodak copier rep shows customers how to use less paper and toner—even though more paper and toner would increase profits and commissions for Kodak.

A leading car repair chain helps customers avoid future problems with their cars by simply providing a written explanation of why something probably broke in the first place.

 The Marriott bellhop who slipped off his dress shoes and lent them to a guest speaker who had forgotten his.

The Nordstrom sales clerk who took a Saturday night cab to deliver a new leather coat for his customer's big date.

And a couple more from the Simple Truths' book *Customer Love:*

 A concierge at the Broadview Hotel in Wichita, Kansas, who calls guests a week before their arrival just to see if they need anything special when they visit the hotel.

A bartender at the Capital City Club in Georgia, unfamiliar with the cocktail called a Sazerac, calls the restaurant in New Orleans where it's the house specialty, to find out how it's made. He then presents the diner with both the drink and the list of ingredients on a card that expresses his pleasure for serving him.

The list goes on and on. Your ability to wow your customers is only limited by your imagination and your commitment to serve. Have fun creating Raving Fans!

"IT IS THE **SERVICE** WE ARE NOT OBLIGED TO GIVE THAT PEOPLE **VALUE MOST**."

— JAMES C. PENNEY

56

RULE #

YOU ONLY GET ONE CHANCE TO MAKE A FIRST IMPRESSION...

WITH BOTH YOUR EMPLOYEES AND YOUR CUSTOMERS

You Only Get One Chance to Make A First Impression…

RULE # 6

A few years ago, I had dinner with a friend and met his wife, Terri, for the first time. Our dinner conversation led to the fact that I had started McCord Travel and she said, "I can't believe it, I used to work for McCord."

She then said, "I have wonderful memories of my time at McCord, and I'll never forget how they treated me my first day on the job." I sold McCord in 1985, and my friend, Bruce Black, stayed on to run the company for the new owner. So, I can take no credit for Terri's special memory.

Terri said,

"There was something different happening from the moment I walked through the front door… more energy and more smiles than I was used to at other jobs.

"I was greeted by a very nice young lady who said that she was going to be my mentor during the first week, and if I had any questions she'd be happy to answer them. She introduced me to the people in each department. At lunch, she presented me with a gift of personalized stationery. **They all went the 'extra mile' to make me feel at home…and, I'll never forget it."**

Robert W. Baird, an employee-owned investment company from Milwaukee, also believes in the personal touch. New hires are greeted with flowers on their desk, and they also meet with the CEO for a new associates' event. The company understands that little things can make a big difference.

212 SERVICE STRATEGY

CREATE A PERSONALIZED GIFT FOR NEW EMPLOYEES

Another first impression idea is to send a note and small gift to the employee's home, welcoming

"GIVING PEOPLE A LITTLE MORE THAN THEY EXPECT IS A GOOD WAY TO GET BACK A LOT MORE THAN YOU WOULD EXPECT."

— ROBERT HALF

him or her on board. This way, the employee's spouse (if they are married) is left with a good first impression as well.

Most leaders grossly underestimate the power of a first impression, not only with their employees, but also with their customers. For example, Marj Webber was my assistant at Successories. Marj was responsible for dealing with the various photography companies that we used for our materials. One day she came into my office and said, **"I've been doing this for a long time, but this is the nicest letter I've ever received."** She said she had just placed an order with Alaska Stock Images and received this letter a few days later. Here's what it said:

Dear Marjorie,

Thank you for your recent purchase. We appreciate the opportunity to serve you and look forward to working with you again. We hope you'll enjoy the enclosed gift.

Satisfied customers are our best advertisement, so I encourage you to give us feedback on how we're doing. If we ever disappoint you, I hope you'll let us know; we'll do everything we can to make things right.

In the meantime, if you have any questions or require assistance, please feel free to contact us.

Thank you again for selecting us. It is our privilege to work with you.

Sincerely,
Laurie Campbell, Alaska Stock Images

Now, you tell me…how long did it take to write this letter and send a small gift?

The answer is not long! But, the impact was powerful and lasting. It immediately separated this vendor from the competition.

> NEVER FORGET, WITH EVERY NEW EMPLOYEE AND EVERY NEW CUSTOMER YOU HAVE **ONLY ONE CHANCE...JUST ONE**, TO MAKE A GREAT FIRST IMPRESSION.

PLAN IT.
MAKE IT ALL IT CAN BE!

"IF YOU WORK JUST FOR MONEY, YOU'LL NEVER MAKE IT, BUT **IF YOU LOVE WHAT YOU'RE DOING** AND YOU ALWAYS PUT THE CUSTOMER FIRST, **SUCCESS** WILL BE YOURS."

— RAY KROC

64

RULE #

IDENTIFY
YOUR MOMENTS OF
TRUTH

Identify Your Moments of Truth

RULE #

In 1981, Jan Carlzon had just been named the CEO of Scandinavian Airlines. His company was in trouble. **They had just been ranked by a consumer poll as the worst airline in the world.** Last in service, last in dependability, and last in profits as a percentage of sales. Yet one year later, in the same poll, they were ranked number one in all three categories. What happened? ✈

Carlzon decided to focus on what he thought was the most critical issue…serving the customer. He wanted to keep it simple:

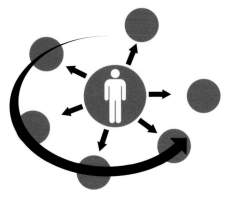

IDENTIFY *EVERY* CONTACT BETWEEN THE CUSTOMER AND THE EMPLOYEE, AND TREAT THAT CONTACT AS… "A MOMENT OF TRUTH."

He set out to let his people know the importance of that moment… the captain, the ticket agent, the baggage handler, the flight attendant.

"Every moment, every contact," he said, **"must be as pleasant and as memorable as possible."**

> "EVERY MOMENT, EVERY CONTACT MUST BE AS PLEASANT AND AS MEMORABLE AS POSSIBLE."
> — JAN CARLZON

He figured that he had approximately 10,000,000 customers each year, and on average each customer made contact with five of his people for approximately 15 seconds apiece. Therefore, in his mind, these 50,000,000 contacts, 15 seconds at a time, would determine the fate of his company.

212 SERVICE STRATEGY

REMOVE
THE BARRIERS THAT
KEEP YOUR TEAM FROM
EXECUTING
YOUR PLAN.

He set out to share his vision with his 20,000 employees. He knew the key was to empower the front line. Let them make the decision and take action, because they were Scandinavian Airlines during those 15 seconds. He now had 20,000 people who were energized and ready to go because they were focused on one very important thing...making every moment count.

What's job number one for any leader so your employees can maximize their moments of truth with your customers?

Remove the barriers that keep your team from executing your plan. The culprits that create the obstacles usually fall into one of four categories:

OUTDATED SYSTEMS

OUTDATED PROCEDURES

OUTDATED PEOPLE

A COMBINATION THEREOF

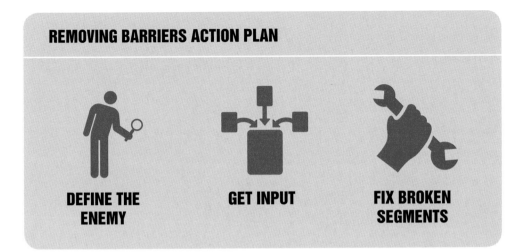

REMOVING BARRIERS ACTION PLAN

DEFINE THE ENEMY   **GET INPUT**   **FIX BROKEN SEGMENTS**

This, of course, assumes that your products are not part of the problem.

The first step is to do some serious diligence to clearly define the "enemy." This requires getting input from everyone, especially those front-line employees who are dealing directly with the customers. Your answers will come if you listen very carefully to what they have to say. Fixing what's broken, however, will take longer especially if the finger is pointed at outdated systems. Fixing problems caused by outdated procedures and outdated people can take less time, but are just as critical.

Obstacles preventing your employees from better serving your customers can vary. They can be 20,000-pound boulders or many small trees. Your job as a leader is to start cutting the trees as quickly as you can so that the people watching will become convinced that good things are about to happen.

> "WHEN YOU'RE UP TO YOUR REAR END IN ALLIGATORS, IT'S HARD TO REMEMBER THAT YOUR PURPOSE IS DRAINING THE SWAMP."
> —GEORGE NAPPER

Focus on what the Customer Experience Feels Like...
FORGET REAL GOOD—REMEMBER FEEL GOOD

I met Tom Asacker four years ago at a conference in Hawaii, where we both spoke. There was one thing he said that I never forgot—"as leaders, we need to forget real good and remember feel good."

For example, he said, there are billions of web pages and 6,000,000 going up every day. There are 89 brands of shampoo at Walgreens!

CUSTOMERS ARE STRESSED OUT FROM INFORMATION OVERLOAD AND CONFLICTING INFORMATION...MORE AND MORE THEY ARE RELYING ON THEIR GUT...AND THEIR FEELINGS TO MAKE DECISIONS.

In fact, he said, it really doesn't matter how customers feel about you and your business. What makes a difference is how your products make them feel about themselves and their decisions. Every psychologist and smart marketer knows that if a man or woman does something and it feels good, they'll do it again; if it feels bad, they won't do it.

"THROW
YOUR HEART
OVER THE FENCE,
AND THE REST WILL
FOLLOW."

— NORMAN VINCENT PEALE

Far too many companies are focused on the product and not the experience. We need to replace our brain with our heart because that's often how people make decisions. Studies have proven that the essential difference between emotion and reason is that emotion leads to action and reason leads to conclusions.

THE QUESTION YOU NEED TO ASK IS, "HOW AM I MAKING MY CUSTOMERS FEEL? AM I MAKING THEM COMPARE OR CARE?"

There's a big difference. **Caring and feelings drive action**…the other stuff is just a tool. The bottom line is that the really hard stuff is the soft stuff…It's the feelings of your employees and customers.

That, in the end, is your competitive advantage.

RULE #

8

Don't Assume…Ask

RULE #

Think you know what your customers and employees want? I'll lay odds that you're probably missing at least one thing that could dramatically improve your business. But there's a simple remedy for that problem—just ask them!

As Jim Williamson, author of *Service: Lessons Learned* says, "Great service is never static, it's always dynamic. That's why customer-driven companies such as Marriott, Avis, Alaska Air, etc. churn out so many customer surveys. Tom Pickett of Sun Microsystems puts it this way:

"NEVER TRY TO FIT YOUR CUSTOMERS INTO WHAT YOU THINK THEY WANT. ASK THEM, AND THEY WILL TELL YOU!"

Here are a few ideas for how to tap your greatest market research source—your customers:

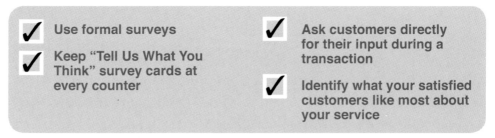

✓ Use formal surveys

✓ Keep "Tell Us What You Think" survey cards at every counter

✓ Ask customers directly for their input during a transaction

✓ Identify what your satisfied customers like most about your service

Don't forget about your dissatisfied customers, too. Survey why they left and more importantly, what you can do to win them back.

LET YOUR CUSTOMERS CALL THE SHOTS

Here's a story that will make you think about investigating what's important to your customers before you spend time and money delivering it.

The only two-time recipient of the prestigious Malcolm Baldrige National Quality Award in the service category, The Ritz-Carlton, manages 36 exquisite hotels around the world. A few years back, they decided to upgrade the bathrooms in their signature properties. They insisted on the best and most beautiful décor. The company invested millions of dollars in design fees. They hand-selected the precise hue, color and pattern of their green marble imported from Italy. After spending millions of dollars and shipping tons of the most exquisite marble across the world, they installed it meticulously in their guest bathrooms.

After all this expense and effort, the company commissioned a research study to ask its customers questions about its service, accommodations and ambience. The results were shocking to the Ritz-Carlton executives. Guests could care less about green marble in their bathrooms; they wanted the bathrooms to be pure white, so they could see it was clean. Their efforts, time and money had gone completely by the wayside.

Bouncing back, management took specific actions to capitalize on the other opportunities for improvement. It revamped its strategic planning process and made it more systematic. It refined and integrated its total quality management.

"LISTENING IS WANTING TO HEAR."
— JIM CATHCART

Goals for customer satisfaction were raised to the "top of the box." Earning a rating of "very" or "extremely satisfied" became a top priority as well as a key element of The Ritz-Carlton strategy —100 percent customer loyalty. In its operations, the company set the target of "error-free" experiences for guests and implemented a quantitative measurement system to chart the progressive elimination of even the most minute customer problems.

THE RITZ-CARLTON CUSTOMER SATISFACTION STRATEGY

EXTREMELY SATISFIED	VERY SATISFIED	SATISFIED	DISSATISFIED	EXTREMELY DISSATISFIED
✖	✖	◯	◯	◯

Steps for quality-improvement and problem solving procedures were identified, analyzed and accounted for. For example, they documented and planned for 970 potential problem instances during interactions with overnight guests and 1,071 such instances with event planners.

"SUCCESS DOESN'T HAPPEN BY ACCIDENT. IT STARTS WITH AN UNWAVERING COMMITMENT TO BUILD A DEDICATED TEAM WHO SERVES THEIR BOSS...THE CUSTOMER."

— MAC ANDERSON

Every day at every Ritz-Carlton, employees from every department worldwide, gather for a 15-minute meeting – called "the lineup," where they review guest experiences, resolve issues and discuss ways to improve service. The meetings revolve around a heroic performance of a Ritz-Carlton employee known as the "wow" story.

Carmine Gallo writes about a family staying at The Ritz-Carlton Bali, who carried specialized eggs and milk for their son who

suffered from food allergies. Upon arrival, the concierge saw that the eggs had broken and the milk had soured. The manager and dining staff searched the town, but could not find the items. The executive chef at the resort remembered a store in Singapore that sold them. He contacted his mother-in-law and asked that she buy the products and fly to Bali to deliver them at once. The family was delighted. Because of the Ritz-Carlton's impeccable system, the story instantly circulated around the world to inspire, teach and remind the 36,000 employees worldwide.

Are your communications and your actions of relevance to your customers? If they aren't, you too, could end up under a whole heap of green marble.

ASK YOUR EMPLOYEES FOR THEIR FEEDBACK TOO!...WHAT DO YOUR EMPLOYEES KNOW THAT YOU DON'T?

There is one question that every employee would love to have you ask...

WHAT CAN I DO TO HELP?

So many times, as leaders, we assume we're doing all we can do; however, these six words: "What can I do to help?" will usually prove your assumptions are dead wrong. The question should address three areas:

What can I do to help you serve the customer better?

What can I do to make your working environment more pleasant?

What can I do to help you better balance your work and family life?

Obviously, it's important to let them know up front that you may not be able to help with everything they ask, but you'll do what you can. In other words, a chauffeur to and from work is probably out of the question.

You'll usually be amazed to hear about a few small things that will cost you next to nothing. You may find they need a new file cabinet, their chair is uncomfortable, they need flex-hours one day a week, a new headset for the phone, or a small space heater for the winter months. The truth is, the fact that you've taken the time to listen to their personal concerns is far more important in their eyes than what you'll do for them. Gallup polled over one million employees who thought they had a great boss and asked them one question. *Why?* You got it! The number one reason was that the boss was willing to listen to what they had to say. Never forget…

IT'S THE LITTLE THINGS, NOT THE BIG ONES, THAT WILL EARN THE RESPECT OF YOUR PEOPLE.

"SERVICE IS NOT A LIST OF OFF-THE-SHELF SOLUTIONS,

IT'S A CONSTANT PROCESS OF DISCOVERY.

TO BE OF REAL SERVICE, ONE MUST BE WILLING TO CONSTANTLY **DISCOVER EXACTLY WHAT THE CUSTOMER WANTS OR NEEDS— AND THEN PROVIDE IT."**

— MARK URSINO, FORMER MICROSOFT DIRECTOR

RULE #

CELEBRATE
SUCCESS

Celebrate Success

RULE #

Some companies just know how to have fun. Take Southwest Airlines, for example. In his book, *Rock Solid Leadership*, Robin Crow tells about visiting his sister, Laura, who worked for Southwest:

"*When Southwest Airlines built their headquarters, they decided to fill their walls with photos of memorabilia. President Colleen Barrett began the tradition of asking employees to submit their own mementos to represent their personal lives and their experiences at*

Southwest. The result is basically an enormous company scrapbook. I saw a cheerleading uniform, an old flight attendant uniform, a crushed tuba (although it did make me think twice about checking my guitar as luggage)—all matted and framed behind glass. Each picture is a piece of what makes Southwest Airlines one of the most extraordinary companies in the world. These halls went on seemingly forever. Imagine it's a five-story building and those photos are on every level, floor to ceiling. It was like the Smithsonian of employee appreciation.

And let me tell you, at Southwest they know how to celebrate. *They know the importance of having fun at work. Laura says that it's not uncommon to see a spontaneous parade marching through headquarters in the middle of a busy workday, or to see a department playing a game of hacky sack in the hallway or testing out their long jump skills. As all of this was sinking in, I began to understand why Southwest's mission statement focused on 'Customer Service, Individual Pride and Company Spirit' over talking about airlines. Southwest Airlines is all about people serving people."*

Having a company culture of celebration is important…sometimes whether you work there or not! I'd like to share Jim Harris' story from his book, *Getting Employees to Fall in Love with Your Company*. In it, Jim talks about participating in Ben and Jerry's contest "Yo, We Want You to Be Our CEO:"

"Some 20,000 ice cream fanatics applied, including me. Although it was a shock not to have been offered an interview, the greatest shock occurred when I opened the large envelope with postage stamped from Waterbury, Vermont. Enclosed was an 8½ x 11 Official Rejection Letter—suitable for framing! This multicolored certificate had a picture of Ben Cohen and Jerry Greenfield, side by side, each wearing a huge top hat emblazoned with the logo of their favorite Ben & Jerry's flavor (White Russian and Chocolate Chip Cookie respectively, in case you wanted to know). The caption read, 'We almost wanted you, Jim Harris, to be our CEO.' *This Official Rejection Letter goes on to say that* 'it warms our hearts—and blows our minds—that someone of your high caliber would even consider a career with us. Your talents and potential convinced us that a much higher calling awaits you. You're just too valuable to the world to be peddling ice cream. Be happy, go lucky.' *But there was more.*

"Also in the rejection envelope was a coupon for a free pint of Ben &

"MEN ARE RICH
ONLY AS THEY
GIVE.
HE WHO GIVES
GREAT SERVICE
GETS GREAT
REWARDS."
— ELBERT HUBBARD

Jerry's ice cream. And there was even more. They also included a 'Call for Kids' brochure that discussed several worthwhile children's agencies that do good work in Vermont, with an encouragement to contact your local agencies to volunteer.

"After laughing out loud at the colorful, outlandish, and brilliantly conceived certificate, and quickly deciding at which store to redeem my coupon, I glanced through the 'Call for Kids' information—and it hit me. *If this is how they treat their rejected applicants, imagine how well they treat their employees! If I was indeed serious about wanting to go to work there, this rejection packet would have redoubled my efforts to join them—in any capacity! With one incredibly fun, insightful, and meaningful mailing, Ben & Jerry's Homemade Ice Cream created both an admirer and a customer for life. Imagine being associated with a company that projects a spirit of celebration and fun that even rejected applicants can participate in!"*

Having a spirit of celebration makes work, well…fun! But, there's something else that all leaders need to keep top-of-mind every day. It's what we all crave…

⤜⤜⤜ RECOGNITION ⤛⤛⤛

A paycheck is what an employee works for. Recognition and praise is what they live for! One of the greatest challenges for managers is finding creative ways to fill that need. Many times, this one thing can be the difference between a good and a great leader.

Michael LeBoeuf understood this when he said,

"The greatest management principle in the world is 'the things that get rewarded and appreciated get done.'"

When creating a recognition program, think about these three main categories:

Formal Awards

These are rewards that are predetermined by management, where employees are formally recognized for their outstanding efforts. They are usually presented in front of the recipient's peers on a monthly, quarterly or yearly basis.

In most cases, organizations will offer personalized awards, such as plaques or engraved crystal. However, sometimes, depending on the significance of the award, other gifts can be given (i.e. trips, watches, a day off, cash).

Informal Awards

Informal award programs are designed to recognize people who have met specific goals. This is immediate recognition given by managers to someone doing something right. They are meant to be symbolic and memorable... not costly. Examples of informal awards can be a departmental celebration, a free lunch, a gift certificate, a coffee mug, and of course...gift books to inspire, and to reinforce your company's values!

Day-to-day Awards

Day-to-day awards are simple acts of kindness, gratitude and

respect. They come in the form of written thank-you notes, letters of appreciation, or positive feedback via voicemail or e-mail. These awards play a very important role in employee satisfaction and loyalty.

Ideas for employee recognition are limited only by your imagination and your commitment to your employees. For example, at the California supermarket chain, Nugget Market, the executive team washed the cars of every associate at an employee appreciation event. At the Johnson Financial Group, if employees fall on hard times, they know that they have the company's support. An associate's salary is kept intact if he or she is out due to a crisis. As CEO Richard Hansen says, ***"JFG will always 'do what's right.'"***

At United Supermarkets, they've used the following to recognize their employees:

Distributing tickets to concerts or local entertainment events and allowing team members to invite family and friends.

Leasing a cabin in the mountains or at a beach, and allowing team members to take their families and friends for a week at a time.

Leasing a private suite for a college or professional sporting event and allowing team members to bring their families.

Providing a team member with a *gift card and a personal word of thanks.*

Sending a team member and his or her spouse *on a romantic getaway.*

Hiring a professional photographer to take a formal family portrait. Have it framed to match the team member's home décor.

Remember, recognition is a need we all crave, and there are no exceptions. So, take the opportunity to celebrate success, reinforcing your goals on a daily, weekly and monthly basis.

YOU ARE MAKING AN INVESTMENT IN YOUR MOST IMPORTANT ASSET... YOUR PEOPLE!

Tom Peters so wisely said... *"We wildly underestimate the power of the tiniest personal touch."*

"WE WILDLY UNDERESTIMATE
THE POWER OF THE
TINIEST
PERSONAL TOUCH."
—TOM PETERS

RULE #

10

REINFORCE.
REINFORCE.
REINFORCE.

Reinforce. Reinforce. Reinforce

RULE #

I'm sure you've heard

the three keys to purchasing real estate... location, location, location. Well you'll now hear the three keys to inspiring 212° Service... REINFORCE, REINFORCE, REINFORCE.

Many leaders in times of change grossly underestimate the need for continuous reinforcement. In a perfect world, we hear something once, record it in our brain, and never need to hear it again. But in reality, our world is far from perfect. During a time of change, we have doubts, fears and occasional disappointments. Sometimes, there are friends, family and co-workers reinforcing those doubts saying,

"IT WON'T WORK."

Once the management team has signed off on the "change message," the challenge is how you can keep it alive until the behavior is consistent with your goals. **Understand one thing — it won't happen on its own.** You need to have a plan in place to make it happen. Answering these three questions is a first step for success:

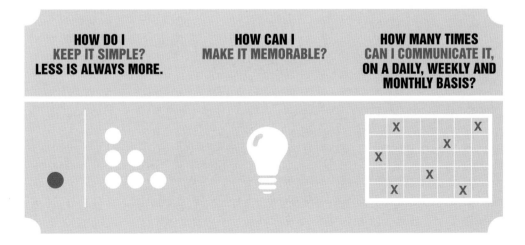

HOW DO I KEEP IT SIMPLE? LESS IS ALWAYS MORE.

HOW CAN I MAKE IT MEMORABLE?

HOW MANY TIMES CAN I COMMUNICATE IT, ON A DAILY, WEEKLY AND MONTHLY BASIS?

To some, this may sound like simple, common sense stuff. But to do it right, it's anything but simple. It takes creative planning and input from everyone involved. But, most of all, it takes tremendous discipline to keep the "train on the track." A lot of little things will make a big difference in convincing the team that you're 100 percent committed to making a 212° Service culture happen. So sweat the small stuff and remember…reinforce, reinforce, reinforce.

MEASURE RESULTS

Most employees want to grow, they want to do better, they want to take pride in their work, but they need targets to shoot for. Unless they have clearly-defined goals, the "path of least resistance" will almost always raise its ugly head.

In the words of Peter Drucker,

"WHAT GETS MEASURED GETS IMPROVED."

Of course, Drucker's quote is true for any business any time; however, during change, it is even more critical.

WHAT ACTIVITIES CAN I MEASURE TO TRACK OUR PROGRESS?

1 Determine area of improvement

2 Set realistic goals

3 Track, monitor and review results

First, of course, you must determine where you are now with each activity you wish to improve. Secondly, you need to set realistic targets for improvement. Thirdly, and most importantly, you must track, monitor, and review results on a daily, weekly and monthly basis. Now this may sound boring, but it is critical to break old habits and to inspire new thinking.

"YOUR SUCCESS IN LIFE
ISN'T BASED ON YOUR ABILITY TO
SIMPLY CHANGE. IT IS BASED ON
YOUR ABILITY TO

CHANGE
FASTER

THAN YOUR COMPETITION,
CUSTOMERS AND BUSINESS."

— MARK SANBORN

Here are just a few examples of what could be measured to track your progress:

What percentage of phone calls are being answered on the first, second or third ring?

What percentage of orders are being processed, and shipped, on the same day, the second day, or the third day?

What percentage of orders have products that are backordered?

In your customer satisfaction surveys, what percentage of your customers are giving your service an excellent rating, a good rating, a fair rating, etc...?

The answers to all of these questions will give you the answer to that question which everyone is looking for in creating a **212° Service Culture...**

ARE WE MAKING PROGRESS TOWARD OUR GOAL?

212° Service

Conclusion

BUILDING THE FOUNDATION FOR A
212° SERVICE CULTURE

Creating a service culture involves changing from the way things have always been done.

In the long run, sameness is the fast track to mediocrity. And, mediocre companies won't survive. Tuli Kupferberg said it best… "When patterns are broken, new worlds emerge." And that is your challenge…to convince your team that the new world you are trying

to create is better than the one you're in. Is it easy? Of course not. It takes planning, commitment, patience and courage. A big part of success, as a leader, will be your ability to inspire your team to get out of their comfort zones; to assure them that even though they are on a new path, it's the right path, for the right reasons.

"WHEN **PATTERNS** ARE BROKEN NEW WORLDS **EMERGE**."

— TULI KUPFERBERG

READY TO GET STARTED?

Keep in mind the "Parable of the Black Belt," as told in the book, *Built to Last: Successful Habits of Visionary Companies,"* by James C. Collins and Jerry I. Porras:

Picture a martial artist kneeling before the master sensei in a ceremony to receive a hard-earned black belt. After years of relentless training, the student has finally reached a pinnacle of achievement in the discipline.

"Before granting the belt, you must pass one more test," says the sensei.

"I am ready," responds the student, expecting perhaps one final round of sparring.

"You must answer the essential question: What is the true meaning of the black belt?"

"The end of my journey," says the student. "A well-deserved reward for all my hard work."

The sensei waits for more. Clearly, he is not satisfied. Finally, the sensei speaks. "You are not yet ready for the black belt. Return in one year."

A year later, the student kneels again in front of the sensei.

"What is the true meaning of the black belt?" asks the sensei.

"DEVELOPING A **212 SERVICE CULTURE** REPRESENTS THE BEGINNING—THE START OF A NEVER-ENDING JOURNEY OF DISCIPLINE, WORK, AND THE PURSUIT OF AN EVER-HIGHER STANDARD."

"A symbol of distinction and the highest achievement in our art," says the student.

The sensei says nothing for many minutes, waiting. Clearly, he is not satisfied. Finally, he speaks. "You are still not ready for the black belt. Return in one year."

A year later, the student kneels once again in front of the sensei. And again the sensei asks, "What is the true meaning of the black belt?"

"The black belt represents the beginning—the start of a never-ending journey of discipline, work, and the pursuit of an ever-higher standard," says the student.

"Yes. You are now ready to receive the black belt and begin your work."

I hope you and your employees enjoy building a 212° Service Culture at your company. I know your customers will!

"Some men see things as they are and say 'why?' Others dream things that never were and say, 'why not?'"

— George Bernard Shaw

Mac Anderson is the founder of Simple Truths and Successories, Inc., the leader in designing and marketing products for motivation and recognition. These companies, however, are not the first success stories for Mac. He was also the founder and CEO of McCord Travel, the largest travel company in the Midwest, and part owner/VP of sales and marketing for Orval Kent Food Company, the country's largest manufacturer of prepared salads.

His accomplishments in these unrelated industries provide some insight into his passion and leadership skills. He also brings the same passion to his speaking when he speaks to many corporate audiences on a variety of topics, including leadership, motivation, and team building.

Mac has authored or co-authored 17 books that have sold over three million copies. His titles include:

17
BOOKS

3,000,000
COPIES

- *212°: The Extra Degree*
- *Change is Good…You Go First*
- *Charging the Human Battery*
- *Customer Love*
- *Finding Joy*
- *Learning to Dance in the Rain*
- *Motivational Quotes*
- *The Best of Success*
- *The Dash*
- *The Essence of Leadership*
- *The Nature of Success*
- *The Power of Attitude*
- *The Power of Kindness*
- *The Road to Happiness*
- *To a Child, Love is Spelled T-I-M-E*
- *You Can't Send a Duck to Eagle School*
- *What's the Big Idea?*

For more information about Mac, visit www.simpletruths.com